The Inner Dialect

Poems

Lennon Stravato

This book is dedicated to William C. Chittick whose wisdom and teachings illuminated my path. After two decades his words continue to echo through my heart and mind.

Praise for "The Inner Dialect"

"Lennon Stravato's poems are, as in his words, vessels of truth, that come from beneath the bone"

- Chris Gantry, musician, songwriter, novelist and playwright, whose works have been performed by Johnny Cash, Roy Clark, Robert Goulet, Wayne Newton, Reba McEntire, KD Lang and Glen Campbell

"This is a book of breath. If you are seeking a bridge to your own sense of spirit, this book is that bridge. Ingeniously spiritual, emotionally powerful…"

- David Dephy, Georgian-American award-winning poet and novelist, founder of Poetry Orchestra.

"This collection envelops you in the most earnest of embraces, ringing true like a song that you forgot you knew every word to, leaving you unshakably certain that we are all connected."

- Jonah Loop, director, producer, storyteller, known for Transporter 2, Collateral, and The League of Extraordinary Gentlemen.

Table of Contents

About the Author

Lennon Stravato is a poet, screenwriter, and producer of Emmy Award winning television. His work situates the human condition at the intersection of the sacred and the tragic. Meaning and meaninglessness are treated as omnipresent and interwoven realities for a being inclined toward, but practically estranged from love, destiny, and the divine.

Lennon studied Religion at Stony Brook University and International Affairs at New York University. You can find him performing his poetry at literary events throughout Long Island and New York City.

From Fevers of the Mind Press Editor David L O'Nan about "The Inner Dialect" by Lennon Stravato

"Inner Dialect" is a captivating debut book by poet Lennon Stravato, whose remarkable talent has made waves on the vibrant New York City poetry scene. With his introspective and evocative verses, Stravato explores the depths of the human experience, touching the hearts and minds of readers worldwide.

One of the most compelling aspects of Stravato's poetry is his unique and profound understanding of the inner dialect that resonates within each individual. He delves into the complexities of human emotions, thoughts, and desires, unearthing the hidden conversations we have with ourselves. Through his skillful use of language, Stravato unveils the innermost conflicts, yearnings, and truths that shape our lives.

The somber tone that permeates the poems in "Inner Dialect" adds a poignant layer of depth to Stravato's work. He fearlessly explores themes of melancholy, longing, and existential introspection, inviting readers to reflect on their own experiences of sorrow, loss, and the search for meaning. Stravato's ability to express these emotions with raw honesty and lyrical beauty captivates readers and draws them into a world of profound introspection.

Furthermore, Stravato's poetic voice carries a distinct dialect that is both intimate and universal. His words capture the essence of human existence, transcending cultural, social, and linguistic boundaries. Whether you are a poetry enthusiast or new to the genre, Stravato's work has the power to touch your soul, making his poetry accessible and compelling to readers from all walks of life.

"The Inner Dialect" is a collection that demands to be read, serving as a testament to Stravato's immense talent and the universality of his poetic vision. Through his somber poems, he invites readers on a journey of self-discovery, guiding them through the intricate channels of the human psyche. With each verse, Stravato's words resonate deeply, leaving an indelible impression and inspiring readers to embrace their own inner dialects, to seek understanding, and to find solace in the shared human experience.

"What lies behind us and what lies before us are tiny matters compared to what lies within us."

- Ralph Waldo Emerson

Unwritten Love

I see you by the old wind chimes
kneeling there beside the bay
just past the hands of time
in a memory that won't decay

Now there's a million pages
fate never chose to write
but if I had my way, then
we would still be side by side

And I drowned your ghosts in bourbon
but found out they can drink
They told me everything and nothin'
are closer than you'd think

So I studied all the ancients
loved with total care
walked the shorelines and the forests
inhaled the mountain air

all to seek relief from reasons
i had chosen to believe
like every bygone season
nobody can retrieve—

But of all the million pages
fate never chose to write
the one that still calls my name is
me and you side by side

Final Thread

I was heading down to Nashville
on the fumes of my last prayer
when I stepped inside an old hotel
and saw a girl with chestnut hair

Her eyes shined like a memory
of all that lay ahead
and what I feared my destiny
might just leave unsaid

She was perfectly familiar
although we never met
I could hear that cosmic dealer
say it's time to place your bets

The lights they quickly flickered
then broke beyond repair
as she came to me and whispered
time makes dust of all affairs

Her wisdom rose like Noah's ark
above my deluge of self doubt
and as our lips met in the dark
the future was announced

It is by fate that we are led
even when we miss the signs
but hanging from my final thread
I knew the time was mine

Street Preacher Paul

Good ole street preacher Paul
always has a smoke to spare
and if he smoked them all
I'm certain that he'd share

the one he now is toking
as he leans in rather close
and says it ain't no joking
there's just one thing that he knows

Heaven is much nearer
than this earth that we call home
If you want to see it clearer
shine that heart like polished chrome

Love is a dimension
beyond the body made of dust
but all our bad intentions
can turn that chrome right into rust

And then we will be blind
to the eternity
that's right behind the mind
of ego's me me me me me

Stranded Light

The soul is but an isthmus
between the spirit and the clay
proclaims my inner mystic
observing now this play

We go on as if it's real
just characters of dust
Yet I feel that we conceal
an otherworldly trust

inherited from far beyond
the stage of images and form
These costumes we have donned
are not roses, but the thorns

I am a candle still unlit
my purpose is to shine
So may these burdens be the flint
that burns my wick divine

I'll lift a glass in grateful praise
to the spirit so sublime
Eternal light, I am a ray
stranded here in time

Broken Diaspora

We fled Toledo pogroms
in search of island peace
My last two coins of bronze
for passage overseas

Soleina played an old guitar
sang the words our forebears wrote
We slept beneath the Azores' stars
our blanket but an overcoat

Until we reached a foothill town
with remnants of our people
Tattered rags as wedding gown
her beauty still unequaled

In those years our family grew
reaching number five
but Spanish ships on trade winds blew
again demanding lives

Our day did start with bloodshed
The evening's offered more
Soleina took the children
I've stayed to lose the war

A Man is Made in Moments

I'm drifting through the shadows
in the January breeze
just thinking of tomorrow
with a hope that doesn't cease

Certain that my seeking
is a burden like the cross
promising a victory
that's bound with total loss

I'm bruising and I'm bleeding
there's no telling if I'll win
but a man is made in moments
where he never does give in

Yes the little ghost inside of me
has managed to endure
the waves of catastrophe
always telling me he's sure

the ocean is much deeper
than the surface where we swim
ignore that old score-keeper
with his undertaker's grin

The fatigue which scars the body
will never shake my faith
even as these trembling hands
can barely wash my face

So I'm bruising and I'm bleeding
but I still believe I'll win
for I was made in moments
that I never did give in

More Than I

I once reached into the ether
for sublime words that I could share
But each one did fall beneath her
to whom my best does not compare

She said: you are drenched in varnish
but all my people have no glare
Hear me, for I birthed the prophets
and you, young man, are not their heir

Well, I trembled at this trumpet
It shook me to my soul
but I was not made to crumble
and instead I raised my goal

I gathered my soul's kindling
and trekked up old Mount Sinai
saying: if you be so willing
have this fire as our alibi

She said earth is temporary
just as those who seek its favor
those you deem extraordinary
were forsaken like your savior

I said I know these truthsayers
and though unfit to walk their path
indeed I've come for this affair
as all, but you, to me is wrath

She said you may join me in this fire
but know that varnish won't survive
there is no room for false attire
if you wish in Truth to be alive

I pledged myself to love, not pride
to live and die in just her name
So here, right now, I'll climb inside
I won't resist this perfect flame

Faith

You said I'm just like Daniel
in that lions' den
but his faith was stronger
so I must be near my end

Well I was born a stranger
and if now it's even worse
I still don't see the danger
so you can go call off that hearse

I've faced so many burdens
and none did take me down
You shouldn't look so certain
that this is my final round

Go bring me your Goliath
with his mighty javelin
I've slayed my share of giants
and I'll leave him to the wind

But when the day is over
and these distractions are all gone
I'll have to make accounts
for the things I have not done

For there's a greater struggle
yes, that one against our fate
to which so many buckle
and refuse to penetrate

Now as for me, I may be losing
but victory ain't out of sight
So never mind this bruising
I'm still in the fight

The 12th Sign

We were standing in the silence
of the words we couldn't say
Dreaming from a distance
about somewhere down the way

past our old and broken roads
and round some future bend
a final turn that could hold
our fates together in the end

Then a decade down a dusty trail
without a moment of her sight
Until that sense which never fails
A ray of heaven's light

And soon from ether to the earth
her message crossed the realms
With a note about my words
came dimensions we could dwell

Now we're dancing in the moonlight
with the rhythm of the sea
that washes this old cliff
we had climbed up just to be

She's a creature of pure nature
returning to its flow
She carries me there with her
where my soul is meant to go

In this perfect presence
where being comes to live
our roads that offered less
reveal their cosmic gift

The wind is spilling secrets
whispered by the trees
Hearts can gently listen
with minds approaching peace

Schrodinger's God

The evening sky rolls through my mind
and opens up my soul
to a glimpse of the divine
no one could ever hold

The cosmos sings an endless song
and we are of its tune
forever dancing right along
but condemned to miss the view

Yet I saw it in a river
of whiskey and lost dreams
when I met my gentle lover
in coincidence that screamed

I felt it in my baby's cry
as I rocked her through the night
with a perfect lullaby
I never planned to write

And now I have returned
to my good old smoky haze
in that line of weary lovers
longing for another grace

Unseen Love

I loved you with a love
you couldn't quite perceive
it stood too high above
the world you chose to see

You'd been busy building
a roof above your dreams
I wonder how it feels
to be imprisoned by those beams

Oh, I prayed that I could reach you
so focused on defeat
but you held the narrow view
where the heart is obsolete

Now I'm forced to recognize
the loss of too much time
So here amid the clear blue skies
I'm off to seek what's mine

I'd tell you that i'm leaving
but I'm already gone
I couldn't wait to see
this darkness meets its dawn

Symphony

We live inside a symphony
you may not know it from the street
I hear the voices of antipathy
that clamor for defeat

But virtue sings a better song
below this choir of conceit
while its days are sharp and long
and forever incomplete

The failures that I take
the losses I endure
though my heart be prone to break
it travels still to yours

From the tension of the strings
come the blessed sounds
No matter what this life may bring
it's love that will resound

Where Streetlights End

We met where streetlights end
in favor of the moon
as her soul began to bend
toward its primal tune

I was then a rising prince
my power did accrue
by having just dispensed
of one accustomed to the view

She disdained fortune's throne
and all for which it stood
I said I'd always known
I'd overthrow it when I could

But soon life sent her east
in search of noble truths
while I had been released
to the many from the few

I traveled broken roads
and faced unending snares
but made a drifter's home
in life's unanswered prayers

Failing fast, left and right
all fortune did depart
except my appetite
for matters of the heart

And in defeat I chose
a different path to trod
above the pain I rose
into the hands of God

Then spirit gave this pen
and told me not to yield
Don't matter if you're broken
the word will be your shield

But now this gust of wind
like a splendid hurricane
has made the pain rescind
and me call out her name

Our love was bright, yet brief
for that was not our time
but in this moment so complete
fate has returned our rhyme

Meeting Her Was Mystical

I saw her in a distant light
that shined so far from me
while deep inside I can confide
I had a sense of destiny

But quite unlike a prayer
that yearns for flesh and blood
a spirit filled the air
which animates this mortal mud

The hands of fate abandoned gloves
to reveal their fingerprints
when she appeared as if to say
this world has no coincidence

I wake up wanting more of her
than time could ever hold
Existence is a mystery
where God himself unfolds

She holds a sense of oneness
through these particles of dust
each of us inhabit
with our otherworldly trust

But I wonder when she reads this
as a cat curls on her chair
will it seem like madness
or a truth that's spoken fair

Eternal Mortality

He negotiates with heaven
for the survival of his son
making every vow he can
but the angels do not come

Doctors slowly enter
with illuminating silence
And as this fate is rendered
a priest falls short of guidance

What is man supposed to feel
about our grand inclemency?
Can I tell him love is real
when he feels no empathy?

I would not blame him for his pain
or offer up immense regret
when mourners linger in the rain
but God has not arrived, just yet

Well the man replied: the hands of time
do not tremble at their duty
to honor the sublime
by betraying every beauty

For every light that shines
in this ragged world of flesh
there is a final line
at which it is undressed

and returned into the haze
from which every form is born
and every anthem, every play
is but a fragment that is torn

Yes, all these that we love
in our mortal brevity
are woven from the fabric of
a true eternity

Café Serenade

In an old café I penned a song
to the beauty of the night,
when by my side, she read along
and said: this melody is endless light

I'd seen her face a thousand times
before we ever spoke
On the muraled wall I saw my rhymes
were present in her every stroke

This little place a sanctuary
where my dreams were safe to grow
And soon they did in harmony
with this girl I longed to know

The wall transformed in heartfelt ways
to honor stranded lives
With each addition that she made,
I got closer to her side

And on a night of thunderous rain
we came to sit so close
her eyes met mine, without a strain
she said: this journey, I have chose

Soon my songs were those of love
to this girl I hoped to keep
but before I could propose
she said: there's something you should see

In the corner's gentle glow
she pulled aside a drape
Revealing on her mural now
a wedding by a placid lake

Nearer than Myself

I rested in these fields
of fragrant old tea leaves
that told me those who yield
will find no cause to grieve

and then the yarrow stalks
I know I heard them say
the cosmos always talks
and guides us on our way

Perhaps all this seems odd
the visions I receive
At times I call it God
but not how some believe

There's no man up in the sky
nor devil down below
and I do not have to die
for this eternal show

There is no distant time
of greater consequence
the heavens always rhyme
throughout my consciousness

The Torch

Say a prayer for the flower
that was warned not to bud
or ever speak of the hour
streets ran slick with our blood

whose Toledo tombstone tears
were only shed at night
through five hundred stolen years
of this unspoken plight

from the mainland to the islands
and then again across the sea
my people lived in silence
but now it's down to me

So for all the Seders in the caves
and the tortured with no graves
I vow that I will shine so bright
the world will know you held our light

Girl from Peasant Row

Upon a throne of other's work
a prince's plan was hatched
while in castle shadows lurked
a girl of cunning, still unmatched

The hands of fate had placed these two
in such proximity
that even God's review
applauded sublime artistry

He blithely spun his royal globe
and pondered where to play
which virgins to disrobe
which valiant men to slay

The kingdom had to grow and grow
to meet his ego's size
but now this girl from peasant row
had sharply focused eyes

What expert marksmen could not do
and deemed impossible
She knew so surely would ensue
if her life, too, was optional

Taking moments breath by breath
she studied heaven's signs
rubbed a poison on her breasts
and said the people's plight is mine

And soon his wealth could not dissuade
the turning of the tide
when in that bed which greed had made
it's said this prince had died

The Image Restored

When she said he supplied
what she yearned for inside
as if the heavens chose him to disburse
he replied, it's just that she eyed
those few things he could provide
and so he felt the reverse
It was in this subtlety
that they heard life's mystery
as the grandest of symphonies, so well
rehearsed

She spoke: it all operates musically
which is just how you speak to me
tell me a word that's not longing to be in your
verse
He said as our ego decreases
I've learned that we're pieces
of a divine puzzle, now broadly dispersed
so that when I found you
there was nothing to do
but finally relinquish my thirst

Now Isn't The Time

Let's choose between these villains,
who has the greater claim
to make dust of some civilians
and find glory in the shame

I think that man of ponderous thought
who's killing fewer than he can
exceeds the one with words of God
that smell exactly like a man

But, perhaps you think the other chap,
for the weaker side should win
Everybody loves an underdog
let's take the devil's evil twin

Oh, who am I to write these words
when sorrow's all around
Stand with those who suffer
Later, conscience can be found

But can you tell me once again
why the world is awash in violence
Is it that the voices true
remain too few and silent?

My Retreat

I'm pulling back the troops
I've chosen to retreat
Put it in your books
call it my defeat

Forty years I've traveled
a member of this play
now it has unraveled
and there's nothing to portray

Nothing to preserve
the chalet and the shop
what idols did I serve
in these ironic props

A body's made of dust
a spirit holds some light
This time I've put my trust
in my vision not my sight

Those who lust for objects
become just what they seek
but he who does reflect
evades this mortal heap

I yearn for that much more
than the mandate of a clock
I've set my heart to what endures
long after it has stopped

I'm calling off the troops
I've chosen to retreat
Put it in your books
Call it my defeat

Matter and Ghost

Sometimes I stop and ask
are we just spirit in an hourglass
but when the answer does not come to pass
this pile of prayer and dust finds himself a
different task

Like looking through that magnifying glass
toward the borders of my mediocrity
fearing I shall never trespass
the limits of mundane geography

When the sand depletes
will my story be complete
or will I have written something that holds
the taste of truth for other vessels

who also avoid rest so they might wrestle
with the question of what truly unfolds

Is my being different from theirs
or is being-itself just housed in different wares
a divine secret, inexhaustibly disclosed

Alchemy

I've been accused of alchemy
making beauty from despair
But the great divine mystery
resides in ordinary air

With subtle meditation
finding life within the breath
we dwell in love's duration
not a fleeting object's death

Yet, if to some my revelation
comes as something of a threat
I'd say their ordination
wasn't worth the debt

The truth remains unburdened
by every prior form
And all that's worth preserving
will withstand this storm

So it's time to see life's meaning
transcends every mold
and when wisdom comes streaming
it's neither new nor old

Cosmos in Dew

I awoke in the morning
as she was adorning
her soul with the word
I said: what are you reading
She said our dreams are receding
And it's about time that you heard
I'm tired of waiting
there's no use debating
I won't have a lifetime deferred
So gather your strength
we're going the length
to reach our visions absurd

I packed my old pen
left the books of wise men
She said the next chapter is written by you
And as she gathered her brushes
I said all your paint touches
shall be both ancient and new
We settled in the mountains
among nature's grand fountains
to find the cosmos reflected in dew

She in this there is spirit
so gently adhere to it
that's what the lover must do

Nostalgic Drive

Pink Floyd in the tape deck
enough gas for the day
Don't know how you worship
but that was once my way

I measured youth in miles
from the village to the shore
I hear my rides are filed
inside of local lore

But at some point Eden slipped
from the rearview mirror's grasp
I don't think I know which trip
turned out to be my last

Today nostalgia drove me back
but I couldn't stay too long
I'm on a different track
singing my own songs

Fare thee well, my old hometown
we had our patch of time
But don't call too often, now
you belong to younger minds

The Dollar and the Clock

Drinking whiskey in the corner
of the tavern round the bend
we slipped beyond the border
of the role reserved for friends

Testing every limit
of proximity and distance
our visions were permitted
to eliminate resistance, till the end

Bodies finally yielding
to hearts that ceased concealing
raging fires deep within
In making love we flew above
the fears that used to win

Oh I have seen the shattered dreams
that fall between the dollar and the clock
but in my soul I've always known
that love, and love alone, comes out on top

Yes, I've tasted pride
and been humbled by
the times I have not won
but at midnight in the mirror
the mind becomes much clearer
than the rising of the morning sun
And past the veil of me and you
our bodies hide a deeper truth
we number only one

So into the sea of tragedy
with all the doubts that have no place
I throw the lies that bind the mind
and confine us here to time and space

I have seen the shattered dreams
that fall between the dollar and the clock
but in my soul I've always known
that love, and love alone, comes out on top

Wherever You Turn

As the music moved to her rhythm
all was revealed that was hidden
and I could do nothing but stare
She said: come dream with me
learn to live fearlessly
God's in this rarified air
I looked around at the rubble
a lifetime of trouble
and knew my approach was threadbare
I abandoned all doubt
finally figured it out
The kingdom of heaven resides everywhere

We traveled to the East
possessing the least
but always had kindness to share
Life's not in the objects
an ego protects
but in how gentle you care
And in her fine courtesy
I tasted eternity

Her being was sweet as a prayer
Though now she is gone
I still sing out her song
The kingdom of heaven resides everywhere

Perfectly Unplanned

I woke up to a nightmare
where I thought my dream would be
She left without a warning
and it devastated me

But down among the ashes
of the things I once believed
was the scent of something tragic
in the space where dreams recede

I found her by the fountain
drowning in self-doubt
Told her life's a symphony
that we haven't figured out

And swimming through the sequins
that shimmered down her dress
I found her heart was still a home
for hopes she can't confess

Now she's crying in the kitchen
says her soul still burns for me
and the destiny she envisions
is a place where we'll be free

But, I'm not burdened by the details
of ordinary rules
the heart goes where it will
and makes each of us a fool

Come lay your head upon the pillow
girl don't speak another word
Filtered by these fears
our thoughts are never heard

Yet in the softness of your touch
your hands against my skin
I can feel we've grown enough
to not let the voices win

So I wouldn't change this moment
for a story I could write
The greatest things that happen
start beyond the limits of our sight

And down among the ashes
of the things I once believed
is that scent of something tragic
in the space where dreams recede

It's Also a Net

I remember her touch,
a transient affection
It was never enough
but, I'd love it again

We'd sit on the bench
so perfectly close
Now it's stand watch,
as the ghost of our ghost

The city is famous
for claiming no sleep
Everyone pacing
through sorrow so deep

Millions of echoes
in a canyon too vast
Chasing a future
that's lost in the past

Down by the river
painting over despair
she said that we're all
only sharing a prayer

It's true in the shadows
where each day's a twin
among the lost lives
that never begin

And perhaps in our tavern
though the melody's sweet
for the accent's still longing
and the rhythm's defeat

Yet the fragrance of chaos
lets us share in a dream
where we understand loss
is less than it seems

When the begging dies down
and the ladies grow bored
they turn up that fire
we had failed to implore

So here's to the nights
that overshadow regret
It may be a vice
but it's also a net

That You May Contribute a Poem

I woke up to a verse, with the promise of a poem
The final words could all be found, where the
soul makes its home
For that I had directions, but not a guarantee
as it is a destination, beyond every "you" and
every "me"

Knowing how each desire, makes a cloud before
the heart
and that by some distance, each cloud is set
apart
I started rather early, as the sun began its blaze,
said goodbye to the departing moon, as it took
its final gaze

Then I made a vow, to abandon ego's greed
as it prefers to chase those dreams, your heart
could never need
I steeled myself with memories of ego's past
concerns,
which so quickly all did prove to have negative
returns

And as the day continued such temptations all
did come
promising money, fame, and pleasure, for such a
modest sum
But now I knew much better, how these all were
lies,
and not to let attractive things enter my heart
through these enchanted eyes

Then soon the world did quiet, and my soul
began to rest at ease
for when I let temptation fade, there was no ego
left to please
And then I saw true beauty, in everything and
everyone,
and every word I could ever need, danced freely
in the sun

And as these lines became complete,
the heart gave me a final message, which it
asked that I repeat
It said to share a glimpse into this other world,
and in so doing to make it known,
that it is the human who is a verse, with the
promise of a poem

First Poem for Leonard Cohen

Because his death was something my heart could
not withstand,
I asked the master for a final poem and offered
up my hand
I said "for many years I've been a student of
your word
and if you speak to me I'll help your voice be
heard"

The master softly said: "did you think those
words were mine to tell?
You must know, I procured them from deep
within that great communal well,
And there, young man, you may go searching,
but if anything's retrieved
well I'm afraid you've got that burden, from
which I've been relieved."

And then the master did retreat back into that
great abyss
from which all beings spring and into which we
are dismissed
But in departing he did leave a final remnant - a
tiny speck of dust
as if to say, that's all a man can give, the
beauty's not from us

So I sat there for a moment, and then found
some fresh new pages,
knowing that is all a pilgrim has, when he goes
to meet the ages
And dutifully I wait here, with that paper and
my pen
and my little promise, that when the spirit
speaks, I'll transcribe all I can

*"Poetry is just the evidence of life. If your life
is burning well, poetry is just the ash."*

-Leonard Cohen

Guided Meditation

Retreat into the woods
and deep inside your heart
see gentle rivers flow
and worldly thoughts depart

No need for any words
just water, wind, and breath
perhaps a singing bird
invites you to connect

to life before the space
that advertisers buy
and every little place
between each you and I

Now sit upon the earth
or on some fallen tree
Quietly observe
the rustling of the leaves

Your heart begins to rest
embraced by nature's peace
There's nothing to address
you're perfectly at ease

Folding and Unfolding

I left my losses at the table
by the life I played away
unfolded this old photograph
of the girl who did not stay

I have made a million fortunes
that all slipped through my hands
chasing grand illusions
that weren't worth a damn

Once a man of many dreams
today I hold just one
To have a simple life, that seems
was here before I had begun

And I searched the whole world over
to find the light I held within
But now in losing everything
I know just what I want to win

So I left my losses at the table
with the hopes that made me stray
Unfolding this old photograph
I'm wondering where she is today

Untamed Melody

She left for all the reasons
he never could perceive
Said settling was treason
to hearts that still believe

in a world beyond the sights
of conformist masquerades
a broken Bill of Rights
and Labor Day parades

Then here she slid right in
to our tavern of the heart
where I thought that I could win
her lover's vacant part

She danced to beating drums
and chants that make you cry
This world could turn to crumbs
by the light of her mind's eye

Churches and old temples
bowed in desperate shame
they could not match the sight
of her enchanting flame

We tangoed down the streets
and all through Buenos Aires
each movement so complete
my heart remains ablaze

Mary

I make a pot of coffee
and I spy the morning sun
Mary glances past me
and puts her bracelets on

She comes and leaves as easily
as thoughts I can't possess
enchanting me a moment
vanishing the next

She's a gypsy, she's a jewel
She's a soul you cannot tame
She's my folly, I'm her fool
and I always call her name

Oh Mary won't you come again
life's no good alone
Eventually the clock will win
and we'll all become unknown

She says unknown is all we are
even side by side
You raise me up and make a star
in the filter of your mind

I say, it's majesty, it's tragedy
we're all a world apart
but beneath that grand catastrophe
is a sense we share a heart

So Mary won't you come again
life's no good alone
Eventually the clock will win
and we'll be totally unknown

Bedouin of the Soul

Tinker with that medicine
tinker with those hymns
recites our lonely bedouin
reporting from within

desert landscapes of the soul
vistas sweet and rare
Behind the mind that we control
he's mapping it with care

A little light from spirit comes
he works some on this chart
music from the funeral drums
the beating of his heart

Time, he says, is more than age
our little lease upon the earth
Before it slips now off the stage
consider what it's really worth

He scribbles in his notebook
no words are absolute
God is everywhere we look
except, perhaps, in my pursuit

The wisdom that I borrow
exceeds my feeble hands
Only man needs signs to show
what is always where he stands

Life does intersect
both sacred and profane
but first your heart must reconnect
to see beyond this dusty plane

The Muse and the Burden

Who measures out these hands
ordained to us at birth
Is it random or is it planned -
a cosmic handiwork?

In the cold and darkest season
I begin to understand
The innocence of Eden
could never suit a man

Springtime turns to winter
before a flower is fairly seen
Youth hears not this whisper
for it dies when thoughts convene

Only from the shadows
can one sense the grace of light
My lover in her evening clothes
makes nakedness a holy sight

Heaven's gate stands just beyond
the deepest pit of hell
I tremble at my little fate
assigned to dig the deepest well

Every man's inadequate
to the work he does behold
Against the sky a narcissist
would know it's time to fold

And even Christ did feel forsaken
high upon his bloody cross
If in days he did awaken
did he still not bear this cost

Holy hand, please come to me,
I who can't believe
in the depth of all my misery
you ever did deceive

Streets of Revelation

Standing in the silence
of the empty streets at dawn
He's locked inside a moment
that feels forever gone

From together chasing fate
to now totally alone
His eyes upon their destiny
hers looking for a home

The buses come alive
The crowds begin to swell
He's smelling like last night
and everyone can tell

Hearing all the whispers
he feels he has no name
only dreams that linger
like sparks that make no flame

How this world of noise
now so plainly spoke,
Where she once saw the sage,
it only sees the joke

But in a breath he does release
these sounds that build self doubt
To find a sense of harmony
in his world so upside down

A sparrow lands then at his feet
this a whisper so divine
Though his journey's incomplete
perhaps it's still on time

And if now as he trods
the time-worn cobblestone
he does not overcome the odds
neither does he feel alone

Beguiled

The fire's burning wild
the wind is howling too
and it seems I'm still beguiled
by nights I shared with you

Your beauty was so envied
my prowess was on view
That's not a place to live
but I'm glad that we passed through

The decade in between
this tangled circumstance
how little it might mean
if I could catch your glance

I wonder if you've changed
or how well I knew you then,
why our spark became a flame
I'll carry to the end

Now there's music down on Main Street
the band still plays our tune
and here you are, right on beat
underneath the midnight moon

Your eyes are spilling secrets
there's no need for a word
but in this shared regret
is a chance to quench our thirst

Come now past the lights
on this night so thick with charm
we have our sacred rites
in each other's arms

Oh the fire's burning wild
the wind is howling too
and it seems I'm still beguiled
by each night I share with you

Graceful Coincidence

I was drowning in a river
of whiskey and dead dreams
She came passing incidentally,
if coincidence is what it seems

I stopped drinking my last dollar,
turned my hope back toward the sky
Then I fixed my worn out collar
and tried to catch her darling eye

Who knows the reason
these things happen right on time
I think that I can hear God talking
in little moments so sublime

She took me through my darkest days
stoked the fire in my soul
But though I prayed in endless ways
I could not pay her final toll

And so I strolled into my old familiar tavern
The dusty seat still waiting in the back
But her sound, so profound, broke my pattern
When the jukebox played her favorite track

Out I ran into the rain
With a special sense of solitude
Not lonesome like the pain
Of distance from her truth

*"In the fury of the moment I can see the
master's hand in every leaf that trembles,
and in every grain of sand"*

-Bob Dylan

Charlie's Song

On the corner by the pawnshop
Charlie sings his songs
I drop a coin into his bucket
and then I sing along

He don't care for patriotism
and our foolish waving flags
life, he says, is worth much more
than who controls a map

Yeah, he lost his way in Vietnam
but his body travels on
Gives the people what he can
although they say he's gone

Yes, on the corner by the pawnshop
Charlie sings his songs
I drop a coin into his bucket
and then I sing along

Well the crowd never gathers
but some people will stare
to him it doesn't matter
he's committed this air

And Charlie may seem a bit naïve
but he sure knows where to stand
So every time that I leave, you better believe
I wonder just who gave who a hand

But on the corner by the pawnshop
old Charlie's time has come
They stick a flag into the ground
and sing a patriotic song

Prayer for the Influenced

She's waking to the demons
she tried to leave behind
A million bad opinions
swirling through her mind

The voices just like vultures
asking if she's dead
from an overdose of culture
that leaves her paralyzed in bed

She glances toward her phone
where the gurus wait for cash
and everyone she's ever known
is dependent on their stash

of filters, fads, and lies
that hide us from ourselves
while the magic's deep inside,
not on any shelves

Deliver her from evil
she will not get there on her own
Everybody's got a devil
lord, that they should have left alone

Yes, have mercy on these tender ones
that wouldn't hurt another soul
this world is like a funeral drum
that always seems to roll

Roses on this Battlefield

My map is made of hallowed ground
my calendar of holy days
God is everywhere that love is found,
and that's not bound by time or space

So come with me into a moment
that is perfectly complete
without a vision of tomorrow
that has something else you need

Abandon all the reasons
to doubt these words I say
Nothing is less tenuous
than this macabre and graceful play

I have heard the wicked symphony
in the land of broken seams
There's not an ounce of mystery
there will be more stolen dreams

You can walk with the apostles
as they followed Jesus Christ
and taste the depths of sorrow
in lives that pass on by

But you can't go on imagining
that truth is somewhere else
don't wait for cruel necessity
to find it in yourself

Divine Ink

Poetry is not respected anymore
A poet is not someone who sits there with a page
And decides he has something to communicate
A poet is someone that knows he is a page
And longs to be a book
A book so well cultivated
the forest could not be offended that it had to die
for the words to live

Poetry is the last refuge of mysticism
It is the final heartbeat of the ages
which modernity has failed to extinguish
The poet holds the final license
to utter the word God, with dignity

Poetry is when, to the human pen,
divine ink is given

Acknowledgments

I would like to express my deepest gratitude to the following individuals whose support has been instrumental in the creation of this book:

- David O'Nan and Fevers of the Mind Press, for their unwavering support, encouragement, and friendship throughout my journey.

- William C. Chittick, my esteemed professor, whose profound teachings on the world's wisdom traditions have not only enriched my understanding but also helped shape and articulate my own thoughts.

- David Dephy, whose poetic brilliance serves as an endless source of inspiration, and whose character embodies the very essence of what it means to be human.

- Chris Gantry, the eternal artist, whose encouragement and artistic spirit have been a wellspring of inspiration.

- Jonathan Silverman, for his continual availability and willingness to be a dedicated reader and sounding board for my work.

- Mary Rymer, for her encouragement and assistance in transforming my words into musical compositions.

- Amy Schildge, who unveiled the lyrical dimensions of my poetry and breathed life into my first song.

- Linda Trott Dickman, for her endless moral support, and for providing the platform for my first public reading, a very memorable feature, and the opportunity to present at her own book launch.

- James Paul Wagner, for publishing many of my early writings, including "Nashville" and "Nostalgic Drive," which are reprinted here

-Veronique Stravato, my dear sister, for her editorial assistance early in my journey, and offering more support throughout my life than I could ever detail.

- Dustin Werner-Fazio, for his continued availability and support, particularly in my transition from a Country genre, back toward the more overtly spiritual dimensions of my writing.

- Regina Perretti, a ray of light, whose encouragement and deep presence, has so often been the catalyst for reopening creative channels within myself.

Each of you has played a unique and pivotal role in the realization of this book, and I am profoundly grateful for your support, guidance, and inspiration.

Learn More from Fevers of the Mind

To learn more about Fevers of the Mind you can find our website at www.feversofthemind.com

Social Media as of this printing is Twitter/X @feversof and editor David L O'Nan @davidLOnan1

Facebook is the Fevers of the Mind Poetry, Arts & Music Group.

Anthologies & Other Books Info on Fevers of the Mind

Fevers of the Mind Poetry & Art Issue 1: The Storm (June 2019)

Fevers of the Mind Poetry & Art Issue 2: In Memoriam (August 2019)

Fevers of the Mind Poetry Digest Issue 3: The Darkness and the Light (November 2019)

Avalanches in Poetry Inspired by Leonard Cohen (October 2019)

Bare Bones Writing Issue 1 (July 2022)

Before I Turn Into Gold: Poetry & Art Inspired by Leonard Cohen (February 2022)

Before the Bridges Fell: Deluxe Edition by David L O'Nan (March-September 2022)

Bending Rivers: The Poetry & Stories of David L O'Nan (January 2022)

Cursed Houses by David L O'Nan (October 2022)

Fevers of the Mind 5: Overcome (August 2021)

Fevers of the Mind Presents The Poets of 2020 (January 2021)

Fevers of the Mind Poetry & Art Issue 6 : The Empath Dies in the End (May 2023)

Fevers of the Mind Poetry, Art & Music Issue 7: Bare Bones Writing II (September 2023)

Hard Rain Poetry: Forever Dylan (art & poetry inspired by Bob Dylan) (June 2022)

Hist Last Poetic Whispers by David L O'Nan (April 2022)

Lost Reflections by David L O'Nan (micropoems) (February 2021)

New Disease Streets by David L O'Nan (November 2020)

On the Highways With Many Miles…to Go! Poetry & Art inspired by Jack Kerouac, Townes Van Zandt, Miles Davis, Bukowski, Gram Parsons, Langston Hughes & more (July 2023)

Our Fears in Tunnels by David L O'Nan (November 2018)

Taking Pictures in the Dark by David L O'Nan (February 2021)

The Blue Motel Rooms Poetry & Art Inspired by Joni Mitchell (July 2023)

The Cartoon Diaries by David L O'Nan (December 2019)

The Famous Poetry Outlaws are Painting Walls and Whispers (originally August 2018, reprint in September 2021)

The Poetica Sisterhood of Sylvia & Anne (Poetry & Art inspired by Sylvia Plath & Anne Sexton) (July 2023)

The Whiskey Mule Diner Anthology (inspired by Tom Waits) (June 2023)

Waltzin' Through Rusty Cages (Poetry & Art Inspired by Elliott Smith & Chris Cornell) (August 2023)

Fevers of the Mind Poetry, Art & Music Issue 8: Inspire (inspired by Audrey Hepburn, Prince, Marilyn Monroe, Lana Del Rey, Rita Hayworth, Ava Gardner & more)

More From Lennon Stravato in Fevers of the Mind

You can find more of Lennon's work with "Fevers of the Mind" in the Leonard Cohen poetry & art inspired anthologies: "Before I Turn Into Gold" and "Avalanches in Poetry" Leonard Cohen and Bob Dylan hold a special place in Lennon's writings. As you can tell from the pieces that were in both of these anthologies

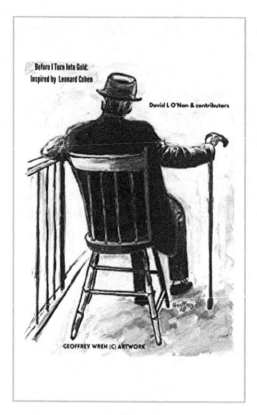

Cover art by Geoffrey Wren

Avalanches in Poetry

Writing & Art
inspired by

Leonard Cohen

David O'Nan

and contributors

ISBN 9781700943460

Avalanches in Poetry

David O'Nan

Cover art by Geoffrey Wren

.

Notes from the Editor:

I'd like to thank Lennon Stravato for coming to Fevers of the Mind for publishing his debut poetry collection "The Inner Dialect"

We worked together as poet and editor coming up with the ideas for the direction of these wonderful introspective pieces that Lennon has compiled.

Lennon continues to amaze us and with this debut poetry collection.

We feel that for you as the reader to engage your mind around the poetry of Lennon Stravato.

We know that you will come away hopeful, realistic, and feeling a little more human as the world becomes more robotic.

- David L O'Nan

The Inner Dialect

First Edition Paperback

Printed in the U.S.A.

Published by Fevers of the Mind Press

©Fevers of the Mind